# Good Morning!

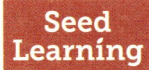

# good morning

# good afternoon

# good evening

# good night

# hello

nice to meet you

see you later

# bye-bye

# Good morning!

# Good morning!

# See you later.

See you later.

# Hello!

# Hello!

# Good evening!

# Good evening!

# Nice to meet you.

# Nice to meet you, too.

# Good night!

# Good night!

# Let's learn about Canada.

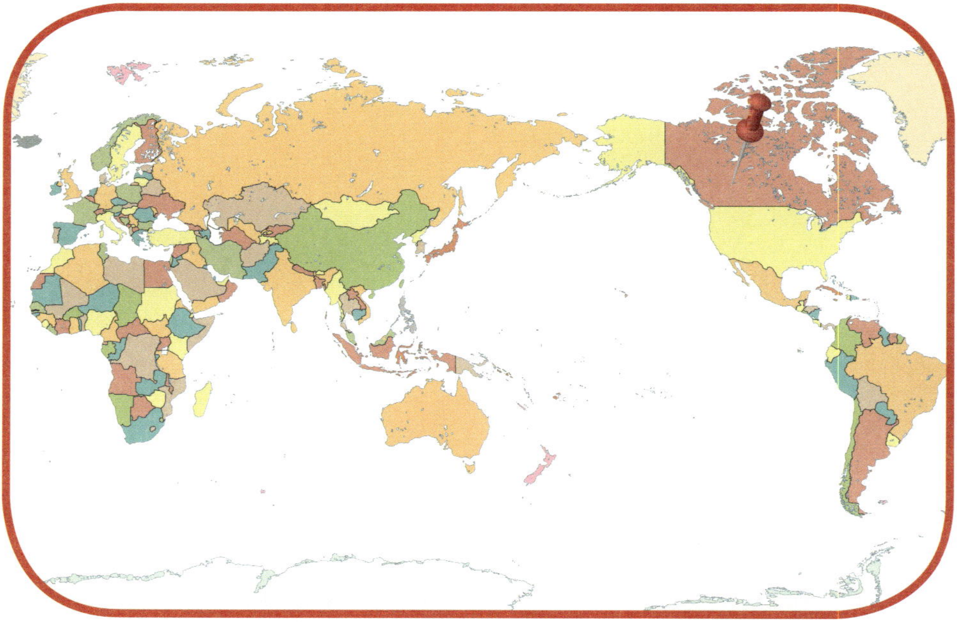

Flag of Canada

Niagara Falls